LOVE

HER

WILD

LOVE

HER

WILD

ATTICUS

poems

HEADLINE

First published in Great Britain in 2017
by HEADLINE PUBLISHING GROUP

8

Photographs by Bryan Adam Castillo Photography, Callum Gunn, Poppet Penn,
or released under Creative Commons Zero license.

Interior design by Amy Trombat

Cataloguing in Publication Data is available from the British Library

Hardback ISBN 978 1 4722 5093 3

Printed and bound in Portugal by Printer Portuguesa

Headline's policy is to use papers that are natural, renewable and recyclable
products and made from wood grown in sustainable forests. The
logging and manufacturing processes are expected to conform to
the environmental regulations of the country of origin.

HEADLINE PUBLISHING GROUP
An Hachette UK Company
Carmelite House
50 Victoria Embankment
London EC4Y 0DZ

www.headline.co.uk
www.hachette.co.uk

For S.R.,
without you
there would be
no words.

'A dream, all a dream, that ends in nothing, and leaves the sleeper where he lay down, but I wish you to know that you inspired it.'

—Charles Dickens, *A Tale of Two Cities*

LOVE

HER

WILD

There is nothing quite
so pure in love
as a boy
and a girl
building castles
in the clouds.

As he took her hand
he gave her
all she had been
waiting for—
a shiver
down her spine.

When it comes to love
we are primates breaking sticks
while pointing to our hearts.

Love
is diving headfirst
into someone else's confusion
and finding
that it all makes sense.

I'll let you into my heart
but wipe your feet at the door.

.

ATTICUS

I think it's beautiful
the way you sparkle
when you talk about
the things you love.

We let our lives
mix with our dreams
like two colored paints
until we didn't know
which was what
and we didn't care.

I want to be with someone
who dreams of doing everything in life,
and nothing
on a rainy Sunday afternoon.

MY
ATOMS
LOVE
YOUR
ATOMS,
IT'S
CHEMISTRY.

ATTICUS

The beautiful thing
about young love
is the truth
in our hearts that it will last forever.

'There's too much risk in loving,'
the young boy said.
'No,'
said the old man,
'there's too much risk in not.'

I promise
to live a life
so rich of love
that at the end
I will not be
so shy of death.

Love is
throwing yourself into a stormy sea
hoping there are arms to catch you
knowing that without the leap
there is only the safe
and lonely shore.

Put a girl in
moonlight
and tell only truths
and every man
becomes a poet.

Love
could
be
labeled
poison
and we'd
drink
it
anyways.

Poetry
to me
is stumbling in the dark
searching for
the right words
to describe
the feeling
I get
when she smiles
while she sleeps.

I JUST NEED
YOU
AND
SOME
SUNSETS.

When I look at you
I find it hard to believe
that the whole universe had not conspired
to bring you to life.
I can't think of a more beautiful reason
for it all to exist
than for you in this day.

Don't worry—
you see,
to some you are
magic.

'If I had all the treasure in the world,
I would follow my dreams,
play with my children,
and spend time with my wife.'
'No,'
said the old man.
'If you followed your dreams,
played with your children,
and spent time with your wife,
you would have all the treasure in the world.'

My sweet darling,
all these tears,
this hurt,
the pain in your heart,
do not fight it anymore,
it is a gift, you see, to feel this much
and even though it's hard
it means you're alive
with each of these tearful breaths gasped
your soul awakens,
more alive in the pain
than you were in the numb,
you are coming back to me now, my love,
lucid in this darkness—
so cry aloud,
yell,
and fall,
and I will be here waiting
to catch you
when the waking up is done.

It took me a long time to realize
that I am happiest
not at the parties
or the dinners
or the shows
but at home with you
and just our books
our movies
and our tea.
And wherever we go
for now and forever
we will bring this happy with us
for home lives
inside us now
wherever
together
we go.

True love comes
when you lose
where you end
and they begin
and the atoms
in your souls
forget where they belong
and slowly you become
pieces of each other
too close now
to ever be apart.

Daughter of mine—
for your smiles,
for your tears,
for your skinned knees,
and your broken hearts,
for the love you give,
and the love you find.
For whatever you become,
or don't,
it is far too late,
I love you already,
long before
we ever meet.

I looked at my mother
and smiled—
she does
so happily exist
in that moment
of one too many
glasses of wine.

Watch carefully
the magic that occurs
when you give a person
enough comfort
to just be themselves.

Does the sun promise to shine?
No, but it will—
even behind the darkest clouds,
and no promise
will make it shine longer or brighter
for that is its fate,
to burn until it can burn no more.
To love you is not my promise
but my fate—
to burn for you
until I can burn no more.

And as I sat and looked at her
and the rolling hills she sat upon
I thought, what amazing luck I have
that the world had created
such beautiful things
and given me the eyes to see them.

The words never meant much
that's not how I loved,
it was when she stroked my hair
when she thought I was asleep
that I knew she really did.

I will follow you,
my love,
to the edge of all our days,
to our very last
tomorrows.

When I saw you first, it took
every ounce of me not to kiss you.
When I saw you laugh, it took
every ounce of me not to love you.
And when I saw your soul, it took every ounce of me.

We drowned out the voices in our hearts
that our love had run its course,
for this night at least
the old music played louder
than the truth that beat beneath our shirts,
and as the stars melted into morning
we smiled at the old stories
and left our love hanging in the air
as we embarked alone
on our tomorrows.

You and I
will be
lost and found
a thousand times
along this
cobbled
road of us.

And the boy told the girl
that he would love her forever—
and she smiled and said,
'but one day we both will die'—
'maybe'
said the boy—
'but I want to
still try.'

IT'S A
LONELY
THING,
PROTECTING
A BREAKABLE
HEART.

It's not the fear of losing them
that scares us,
it's that we have given them
so many of our pieces
that we fear losing
ourselves
when they are gone.

We were strange in love
her and I
too wild to last,
too rare to die.

Do not fall in love with me
for I will break your heart
long before you realize
you were going to break mine.

I let her go
because I knew she could do better
and now she's gone
I wonder
if I should've
just been better.

Love
is a strange magic,
where death
can only make it stronger
while the softest kiss
in the wrong direction,
can steal it away forever.

We so often want
love to work
but we are
fighting currents
of our hearts
that flow
a different way.

WORDS

WILL

SCRATCH

MORE

HEARTS

THAN

SWORDS.

ATTICUS

Obsession is not love,
infatuation is not love,
when someone ignores you
or treats you poorly, carelessly,
or with indifference
that's not love—
that's a lack of love,
for yourself, for trying to fill
your missing pieces with theirs
but when someone is whole
and you are whole
and you act in kindness and benevolence, vulnerability
through strength,
love becomes an exchange
with another person—
and that is
its truest form.

Even those we love the most
can be a poison to our souls.

Break my heart
and you will find yourself inside.

In all the wild world,
there is no more desperate creature
than a human being
on the verge of losing love.

Tell me,
she said,
about our house
our children
our garden
about the lives we will have—
but he never could
and it wasn't until she was gone
that he understood
that she never needed the house
she only needed the dream.

ATTICUS

What an impossible thing,
breaking up,
whispering promises
to ourselves
that other shores exist
and then blindly
wading out to sea.

WE LEFT
OUR LOVE
IN ASH
WHERE A
MIGHTY FIRE
ONCE
HAD
ROARED.

New love is the best cure
for old love gone bad.

I aspire to be
an old man
with an old wife
laughing at old jokes
from a wild youth.

I have seen your
darkest nights
and brightest days
and I want you to know
that I will be here
forever
loving you
in dusk.

Come, my darling,
it is never too late
to begin
our love again.

HER

'I don't believe in magic,'
the young boy said,
and the old man smiled,
'You will, when you see her.'

SHE LIVED IN ME
LIKE THE FIRST FEW DAYS
OF SUMMER:
WARM
AND NEW
AND
INFINITELY
POSSIBLE.

From
the moment
I saw her
I knew
this one
was worth
the
broken
heart.

I took her hand,
and my heart beat fast
as her warmth swallowed me up.
A thousand times I'd run this trail
but not with her.
Her eyes were all that young love should be,
and they lit me up
in every look.
We lay in shooting skies
and freckled stars, and
promised our love would last forever—
and so in our forever
it would
there in a castle atop of Blueberry Hill,
with silver moon rivers
and sailing ships.

Every girl,
if you leave her alone
long enough,
will
eventually
sing
and dance.

She was incandescently beautiful
and beauty was the least of her.

She wore nothing
but the moonlight,
I wore nothing
but a smile.

And the stars blinked
as they watched her carefully
jealous of the way she shone.

She was love at first sight to the
blind man in the dark cave.

A few drinks and the world was hers—
she wore her whiskey like a loaded gun.

She wanted to be rich
and she looked good on a yacht
but I wanted a girl
that looked good by a campfire
with freckles like sparks
to stain
the ashy sky.

I SIPPED
THE MOONLIGHT
FROM HER LIPS
AND STUMBLED
HOME DRUNK
OFF
THE
TASTE OF
HER.

A storm was coming
but that's not what she felt.
It was adventure on the wind
and it shivered down her spine.

She walked
through her life
tired
from the
mighty wings
upon her back.

She flirted with life
and life flirted right back with her,
as if all the universe
came more alive
just for her
and everything felt her glow.
It was
in the dew
in the stars
and the colors of the sky—
they all shone
bright as they could
in the hopes
to catch her eye.

There was a whole magnificent soul
burning brightly behind her '*shy.*'

It was never the way she looked
always the way she was
I would have fallen in love with her
with my eyes closed.

I fought
my eyes to stay awake
no dream was prettier
than the way she slept.

She was afraid of heights
but she was
much more afraid
of never flying.

I promised
to kiss her
a million times
before I died,
fifty a day
for the rest of my life—
so when I was gone
she could smile
knowing
there wasn't a place
on her I missed.

All of the light
all of the trees
all of time
all spinning throughout the darkened sky
as if
the whole world
was created
just to hold her—
asleep on the couch
in the morning sun.

She was that wild thing I loved.
My dark between the stars.

SHE TORE POEMS
FROM MY FLESH,
IN FIGHTS,
IN LOVE,
AND SEX.

She didn't want love,
she wanted to be loved—
and that
was entirely different.

She was the most beautiful
complicated
thing
I'd ever seen—
a tangled mess
of silky string—
and all I wanted of life
was to sit
down
cross-legged
and untie
her
knots.

In this world of bits and pieces
she was whole
so entirely in front of me
the one honest gift
of my life
dripping there
in the rain.

Brushing a girl's hair
behind her ear
once a day
will solve more problems
than all those
therapists
and drugs.

The world is made up of
too many girls
wondering
if they are pretty
and too many boys
too shy to tell them.

I loved her most,
for all the things she hated
about herself,
for that is what
made her different,
and it was the different
that I loved.

She was just another broken doll
dreaming of a boy with glue.

She sat in her perfect house,
with her perfect husband,
wishing that her perfect life
would end.

They saw in her
a bright star burning,
and basked in the heat of her flame,
but behind the bright
she was smoldering
for breath
in the black of a life
she never asked for.

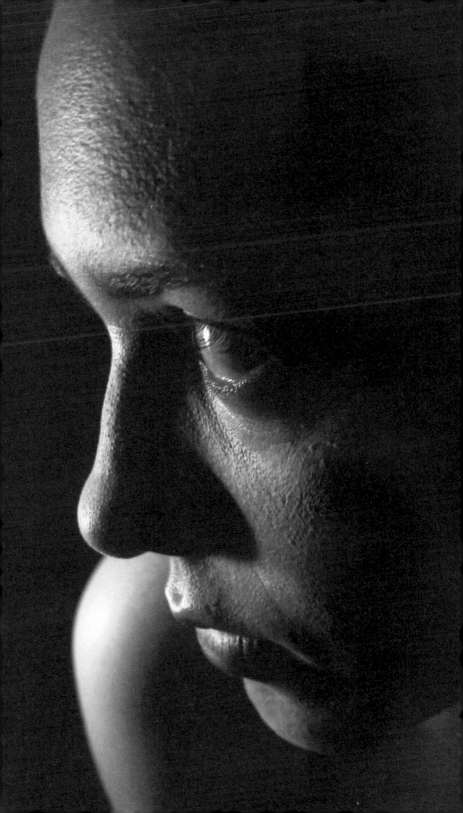

It didn't matter that she fell apart,
it was how she put herself back together.

She beat on against his sky
with forbearing wings,
and with
him gone
she soared
into who she always was.

SHE FOUND HERSELF

OVER A LONG

AND TREACHEROUS ROAD

AND THE MORE

TREACHEROUS

THE ROAD BECAME,

THE MORE OF

HERSELF

SHE FOUND.

Her soul dwelled
in the wild parts
of her heart
vibrating
to the music
it found there.

She sometimes talked aloud
when she thought I couldn't hear
about how she felt
or what she thought
and I would just listen
and fall in love
again and again
from the inside out.

Don't ask her to be a rock
for you to lean upon
instead, build her wings
and point her to the sky
and she will teach you both to fly.

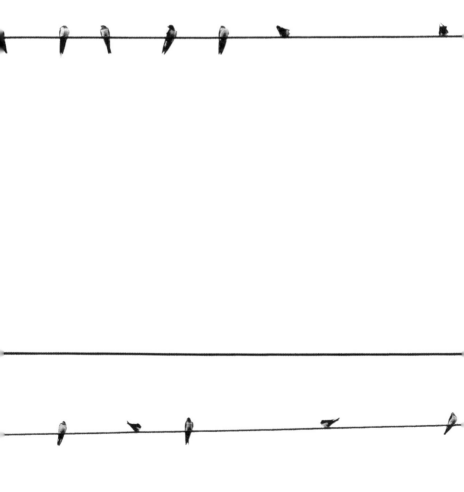

Angels must be warm to fly—
that's why she always
slept in socks.

To me
she is
those final steps
the turn around the last bend
and a little house
with a light on
and a fire lit
with a faint laugh
floating on the warm wind—
she is
my always,
coming home.

I'd always watch
as the world
fell in love with her
I'd smile at the inevitability of it all.
And it wasn't just the boys
the girls loved her more
they'd grab her hand
and run her away
to drink beneath the stars—
they needed to discover
what I already knew—
if she kissed
better than
the champagne.

She was cool—
the whole world
seemed
to spin around her
in smooth jazz.

Her heart was wild
but I didn't want to catch it
I wanted to
run with it
to set mine free.

There is nothing
prettier in the
whole wide world
than a girl
in love
with every breath she takes.

She was too busy wishing
on shooting stars
to see the dreams
come true around her.

She had been through hell
and though no one could see her demons
they could see the face
that conquered them.

She wasn't waiting for a knight—
she was waiting for a sword.

That was her magic—
she could still see
the sunset
even on those
darkest days.

I LIVE

MY LIFE

SO

HAPPILY

IN

CRAZY

WITH

HER.

I feel
like girls
who drink
whiskey
tell
good
stories.

A sky full of stars
and he was staring at her.

It
was
her
chaos
that
made
her
beautiful.

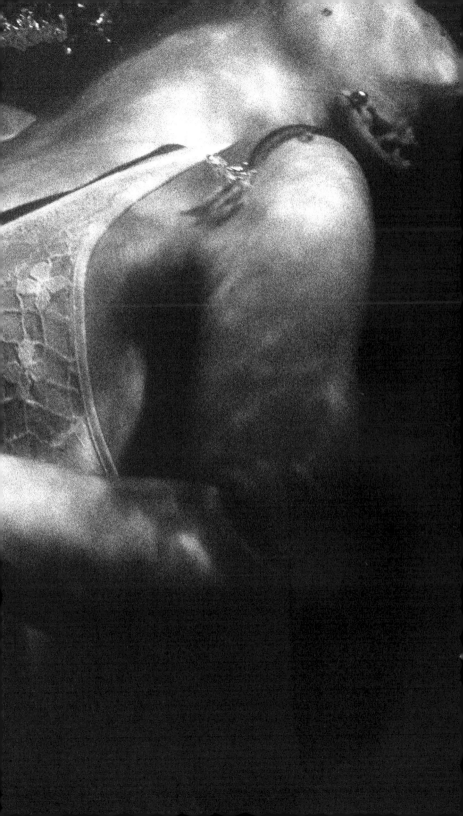

WILD

Chase your stars fool, life is short.

I would rather
have a body full of scars
and a head full of memories
than a life
of regrets
and perfect skin.

Youth came over me like a mad storm.
I was helpless to the chemicals
roaring in my brain.

Our poems
were notes
left behind
to a
confused
younger
self.

Keep your bustling cities,
give me only the moon,
some wine, and old friends
laughing in the desert,
and I will show you
what the
pagans
called god.

Sometimes
I want a quiet life
other times
I want to go
a little bit
fucking Gatsby.

AN ASHTRAY

WITH A GOOD STORY

MAKES THE SMOKE TASTE BETTER.

So many of us
are starving for life
and have no idea
until the end
when we look back
and see the
uneaten banquet.

The world's perception of you
exists only in memories.
Give them new ones.

Drugs
to me
have always been
a pretty girl
with a sly smile
beckoning me
with a finger
down the dark path
of a fork in the road.

I was drunk
on her
laugh,
and the
moonlight,
and the
rum.

A good muse
gives you calm seas
in the morning
and storms
at night
to make you kiss the shore.

We are astrologers
of bodies and mind
searching for truths
in each other's stars.

There are beautiful words
on that blank paper
you hold in your hand,
use the magic
swirling in your mind
to paint the pictures that you see.

FIND SOMETHING

THAT MAKES

YOU

FORGET TO EAT

AND SLEEP

AND DRINK

AND THEN DO IT

UNTIL YOU DIE

OF THIRST.

Go forth and conquer
for the world is small
and you are a giant
and every step
you take
will make the ground shake
as it rises
to meet you.

To him
the horizon was just a slight curve
fading out behind the last tree line,
begging to be straightened
by a quickly embarked adventure.

We
are
never
alone
we are
wolves
howling
to the
same moon.

SHE WASN'T
BORED,
JUST RESTLESS
BETWEEN
ADVENTURES.

The trees seemed to breathe more at night.
There was a freshness in the air
like the world was being born again.
Steam billowed from the machine
and danced up
mixing with my breath.
I rode on into the black,
leaves scurrying from the tires,
startled by this strange one-eyed beast.
I always wanted to remember these moments,
alone on the road
the smell of wood burning somewhere,
and wet cut grass covered with tomorrow's dew.
Fast I'd ride,
deep into the ghostly night,
wind in my face,
eyes screaming tears,
blurring the sky into diamonds,
and my engine,
in its symphony,
became my silence,
a knife's edge to the numb world
my blissful blurry road.

The hardest step
we all must take
is to blindly trust
in who we are.

We humans
are so tortured
by not properly guessing
what will make us happy.

What
a strange
world.
We
trade our days
for things.

I've always liked boxing,
there's nothing like
a punch in the face
to remind you
you don't want to die.

Every word he wrote stood in proud protest to this
most organized world.

Poetry's magic
is that it is found when it's needed.

Art takes time—
Monet grew his gardens
before he painted them.

She made gentle the wild oceans of my soul.

ATTICUS

New York
is the quietest city
I know,
only among
a million beating hearts
could you still hear
the cigarette burn
on a balcony
in Brooklyn.

Hidden away above two thin staircases
a bed, a desk, and bookshelf,
a writer's paradise
the rain would fall and set
its cadence to my thoughts
the old radiator pumped hot breath
forcing my window to be cracked a pinch
and there each night I would fall asleep
in a melody of cold and hot—
wrapped up safe in all my ghosts.

One day I'll paint the perfect sunset —
if I can only find the words.

I think sometimes
of the great stories lost
to old basements,
floods,
and fires,
it makes me sad
until
I think also
of all the stories
not yet made,
in young minds,
in full pens,
and on paper
not yet printed.

Poetry is a lifelong war waged
against ineffable beauty.

BOYS

LEARN TOO LATE

THAT BEING

'THE MAN,'

IS NOT THE SAME THING

AS BEING

A MAN.

We are all born free
and spend a lifetime
becoming slaves
to our own
false truths.

I worry there is something broken in our generation,
there are too many sad eyes on happy faces.

There
is always
a glimmer
in those
who have been
through the dark.

Loneliness
is a fire
I hold close to my skin,
to see how much pain
I can stand
before running
to the water.

Depression is being color blind and constantly told how colorful the world is.

Don't give up now,
chances are
your best kiss
your hardest laugh
and your greatest day
are still yet to come.

Even the bravest wolf hunts with his head down.

ATTICUS

198

We are made of all those who have built and broken us.

POETS

AND

MOTORCYCLES

DON'T MIX;

IT NEVER PAYS

TO DRIVE FAST

WHEN

YOU HAVE HAD

TOO MUCH

TO FEEL.

ATTICUS
⚬
201

True art
comes
from flying
with the madness
so close
you burn
your eyelashes.

Some write for fun
others write
because if they didn't
the words
would grow
and fester
and burst from the seams
of their souls.
Some words
are safer down
on paper.

We all wear masks,
some with makeup
some with smiles
some with wives or husbands
cars or clothes
we hide from the world
and from ourselves
we hide from our truths
behind our eyes
running always from our real
but somewhere there
where truth meets courage
we are waiting to be found

waiting to stand to the world
masks down
and say loudly and boldly
this is us
this is our truth
this is everything real about me
and when that day comes
if it is true
we will begin our lives again
the way they were intended
when the world first
saw our face.

Let my death be a long and magnificent life.

Don't fear,
her father said,
sometimes
the scary things
are beautiful as well
and the more beauty
you find in them
the less scary
they'll become.

All life is a revolt against death
and all revolts are eventually quelled.
The question is:
in those moments
with a rock in your hand
and tear gas in your eyes
can you smile to the fates
stand tall
and
make your voice heard?

There is an island I know
I shouldn't even mention—
it's a fairy tale, you see
where no one wears shoes
and no one needs to—
the houses are hobbit-like
with grass on the roofs
and the food is fresh from a nearby farm
every morning the tea sits steeping
on long wooden counters
with toast and jams from local berries—
the crickets always crick here
and the birds call, the kind
that make you stop and say,
'Now that is a beautiful song'—
the sun is hot
without a cloud in the sky
and the beach runs out for a mile
in silky white sand

so that when the tide flows back in the afternoon
it heats up, warm as a bath,
when it rains
you build puzzles, and paint, and read
and light fires that crackle
and smell like cedar saunas
and each night, rain or shine,
you drink wine
and listen to records
while you play games—
and sometimes
you'll lay in long grass
and chase the stars around the sky
heads close together with the ones you love—
each day is the same
you do what brings you peace—
and the wildest part of it all
is the island is real
my toes are in its sand.

I woke up
from the daydream
of my twenties
in a cold sweat,
anxious for
all the lives
I hadn't lived.

Promise me
you won't die
having never skinny-dipped
in the moonlight
of a summer's night.

We leave behind our unicorns—
the ones that get away—
but they're never fully gone,
they will always be there,
roaming
in the grassy fields of our soul.

In life
I plan to keep going,
till everyone's left,
the band has gone home,
the cleaners have cleaned,
and it's just me and an old friend
daring each other to steal things.

OUR

SONGS

LIVE

LONGER

THAN

OUR

KINGDOMS.

I hope to arrive at my death
late,
in love,
and a little drunk.

What of the firefly,
the one I love to chase?
The old man smiled
Love her
he said
but leave her wild,
and the old oak tree I love to climb?
Love her, he said, but leave her wild
the bird that sings that song I love?
Love her, he said, but leave her wild
and the wolf that cries to the old joke moon?
Love her, he said, but leave her wild
and the horse that loves to run with storms?
Love her, he said, but leave her wild.
And what of *her*,
the one I love most?
And the old man smiled.
Yes, he said,
you must love her too
but love her wild
and she'll love you.

ACKNOWLEDGMENTS

Thanks to:
Penni Thow
Sarah Cantin
Andrea Barzvi
Dave Lingwood
Karlie Kloss
Shay Mitchel
Kaitlyn Bristowe
Spencer Roehre
Joey Parris
Andrew Lutfala
Monarch Publishing
Lindsay O'Connell
Callum Gunn
Ben Nemtin
Jonathan Penn
Jessica Severn
Marissa Daues
Bryan Adam Castillo
The city of Paris
The city of Oxford
Mom, dad, brothers, and sisters.

Everyone at Atria Books and Simon & Schuster:

Emma Van Deun

Albert Tang

Amy Trombat

Lisa Sciambra

Jackie Jou

Suzanne Donahue

Lisa Keim

Judith Curr

I owe a large debt to many writers who have come before me. In particular, the poem on page 53 was inspired by a favorite Hunter S. Thompson quote: *'One of God's own prototypes. . . . Too weird to live, and too rare to die.'* I've always loved the idea of being 'too rare to die'—it's a theme that reappears often in my work—and in this poem, I tried to reimagine Thompson's original meaning.

Thank You,
xx
Attlens